Rose,
Forever grateful,
& love you - Faye

Your Chatter Matters

Margaret Martin

Your Chatter Matters

Journal of Gratitude

Margaret Martin

Copyright 2016

Library of Congress Cataloging-in-Publications Data

Margaret Martin

Your Chatter Matters – Journal of Gratitude by Margaret Martin

ISBN 978-0-9979552-2-4

Published in the United States of America

Cover Design by Meg Lokey

CSP

Published by Conscious Shift Publications
Conscious Shift Publishing Registered Offices: Saint Petersburg, FL 33710

Journal of Gratitude

What is gratitude?

Gratitude is basically being thankful, appreciative or grateful for something that happened in your life and/or someone doing something nice for you; these are a few examples. Research shows us that if we keep an attitude of gratitude we tend to live a happier life. I don't know about you, but I want to enjoy a happy life.

Writing down my gratitudes on a daily basis is something that I have done for over twenty years and I always encourage people to develop this habit. I often post gratitude reminders on social media and in my email newsletter. There is a section it in my book, *The Chatter that Matters ... Your Words ARE Your Power*, dedicated to writing gratitudes.

You may use this journal as you desire. If you are open to embracing the habit of writing your gratitudes daily – I applaud you.

Here's the process I use: I keep a journal on my bedside table and each night right before I turn out my light, I write the date and then three to five things about that particular day for which I am grateful.

Yes, some days it can be a challenge to think of something wonderful however, those are the evenings to remind yourself of your comfortable bed, safe home, your good health, and other blessings.

I look for the simple pleasures of gratitude such as a conversation with a good friend, kind note from a client, time with my family, green traffic lights on my commute, and so on. Once in a while, it is also a good idea to write as many things as you can think of for which you are grateful.

I am very excited to bring this journal to you and hope that you enjoy it.

Margaret Martin
2016

"We first make our habits, and then our habits make us."

\- Charles Noble

"If you have knowledge, let others light their candles with it."
- Winston Churchill

"I have observed that folks are about as happy as they make up their minds to be."   - Abraham Lincoln

_____

_____

_____

_____

_____

_____

_____

_____

_____

_____

_____

_____

_____

_____

_____

_____

_____

_____

_____

_____

_____

_____

_____

_____

_____

"Change your thoughts and you change your world."
- William James

"One of the best things a man can have up his sleeve is a funny bone."

— Anonymous

_____

_____

_____

_____

_____

_____

_____

_____

_____

_____

_____

_____

_____

_____

_____

_____

_____

_____

_____

_____

_____

_____

_____

_____

_____

_____

"Things turn out best for the people who make the best of the way things turn out." - John Wooden

"Character is what you have when nobody is looking."
\- Marie Dresslar

_____

_____

_____

_____

_____

_____

_____

_____

_____

_____

_____

_____

_____

_____

_____

_____

_____

_____

_____

_____

_____

_____

_____

_____

"Joy is a net of love by which you can catch souls."
- Mother Teresa

"Bravery is believing in yourself and that is something no one else can teach you." - El Cordobes

_____

_____

_____

_____

_____

_____

_____

_____

_____

_____

_____

_____

_____

_____

_____

_____

_____

_____

_____

_____

_____

_____

"If a fellow isn't thankful for what he's got, he isn't likely to be thankful for what he's going to get." - Frank A. Clark

"Our problem with change is not our inability, but out resistance."

\- Al Schneider

"One can never consent to creep when one feels an impulse to soar."
- Helen Keller

"Don't compromise yourself. You are all you've got."
- Janis Joplin

_____

_____

_____

_____

_____

_____

_____

_____

_____

_____

_____

_____

_____

_____

_____

_____

_____

_____

_____

_____

_____

_____

_____

_____

_____

_____

_____

_____

_____

_____

_____

_____

_____

_____

_____

_____

_____

_____

_____

_____

_____

_____

_____

_____

_____

_____

_____

"Life is like playing a violin solo in public and learning the instrument as one goes." - Samuel Butler

"Faith is not belief without proof, but trust without reservations."

\- Elton Trueblood

_____

_____

_____

_____

_____

_____

_____

_____

_____

_____

_____

_____

_____

_____

_____

_____

_____

_____

_____

_____

_____

_____

_____

_____

_____

_____

_____

_____

_____

_____

_____

_____

_____

_____

_____

_____

_____

_____

_____

_____

_____

_____

_____

_____

_____

_____

_____

_____

_____

"It is not easy to find happiness in ourselves, and it is not possible find it anywhere else." - Agnes Repplier

"Accept the gift you have given to so many. Let people love you back."
- Jeanette Osias

_____

_____

_____

_____

_____

_____

_____

_____

_____

_____

_____

_____

_____

_____

_____

_____

_____

_____

_____

_____

_____

_____

_____

_____

_____

_____

_____

_____

_____

_____

_____

_____

_____

_____

_____

_____

_____

_____

_____

_____

_____

_____

_____

_____

_____

_____

_____

_____

_____

_____

_____

_____

_____

_____

"Have patience with all things, but first of all with yourself."
        - St. Francis De Sales

"Keep yourself well-oiled with life, laughter, new ideas, and action. Otherwise, you'll rust out." - Anonymous

_____

_____

_____

_____

_____

_____

_____

_____

_____

_____

_____

_____

_____

_____

_____

_____

_____

_____

_____

_____

_____

_____

"Imagination is more important than knowledge."
\- Albert Einstein

"To live a creative life, we must lose our fear of being wrong."
— Joseph Chilton Pearce

_____

_____

_____

_____

_____

_____

_____

_____

_____

_____

_____

_____

_____

_____

_____

_____

_____

_____

_____

_____

_____

_____

_____

_____

_____

_____

_____

_____

_____

_____

_____

_____

_____

_____

_____

_____

_____

_____

_____

_____

_____

_____

_____

_____

_____

_____

_____

"The ultimate lesson all of us have to learn is unconditional love, which includes not only others, but ourselves as well." - Elizabeth Kübler-Ross

"Life is what we make it, always has been, always will be."
- Grandma Moses

_____
_____
_____
_____
_____
_____
_____
_____
_____
_____
_____
_____
_____
_____
_____
_____
_____
_____
_____
_____
_____
_____

"If the only prayer you ever say in your entire life is thank you, it will be enough." - Meister Eckhart

"You can't copy anybody and end up with anything. If you copy, it means you're working without any real feeling." - Billie Holiday

_____

_____

_____

_____

_____

_____

_____

_____

_____

_____

_____

_____

_____

_____

_____

_____

_____

_____

_____

_____

_____

_____

_____

"You will do foolish things, but do them with enthusiasm."
- Colette

"In the middle of difficulty lies opportunity."
  - Albert Einstein

"Life is change. Growth is optional. Choose wisely."
  - Karen Kaiser Clark

"Truly, it is in the darkness that one finds the light, so when we are in sorrow, then this light is nearest of all to us." - Meister Eckhart

"Music produces a kind of pleasure which human nature cannot do without."   - Confucius

"One word frees us of all the weight and pain of life: that word is Love."
- Sophocles

"When you are content to be simply yourself and don't compare or compete, everybody will respect you." - Lao-Tzu

"Work keeps us from three great evils: boredom, vice and poverty."
    - Voltaire

_____

_____

_____

_____

_____

_____

_____

_____

_____

_____

_____

_____

_____

_____

_____

_____

_____

_____

_____

_____

_____

_____

_____

_____

_____

_____

_____

_____

_____

_____

_____

_____

_____

_____

_____

_____

_____

_____

_____

_____

_____

_____

_____

_____

_____

_____

_____

_____

_____

"There is no progress without some discomfort."
- Unknown

"Let your heart soar as high as it will. Refuse to be average."
- A.W. Tozer

_____

_____

_____

_____

_____

_____

_____

_____

_____

_____

_____

_____

_____

_____

_____

_____

_____

_____

_____

_____

_____

_____

_____

_____

_____

_____

_____

"Worry = useless consumer of time, energy and attitude."
                                                    - Margaret Martin

"Love deeply and passionately. You might get hurt, but it's the only way to live life completely." - Unknown

_____

_____

_____

_____

_____

_____

_____

_____

_____

_____

_____

_____

_____

_____

_____

_____

_____

_____

_____

_____

_____

_____

_____

"Everyone thinks of changing the world, but no one thinks of changing himself." - Leo Tolstoy

"Unconditional self-acceptance is the core of a peaceful mind."
- St. Francis de Sales

_____

_____

_____

_____

_____

_____

_____

_____

_____

_____

_____

_____

_____

_____

_____

_____

_____

_____

_____

_____

_____

_____

_____

_____

_____

_____

"Try not to become a person of success, but rather to become a person of value."
- Albert Einstein

"Hold on to your dreams:
Ask questions | Plan to succeed | Proceed with confidence
Invest in the right attitude |Never stop believing | Enjoy the detours
Save time for little things | Share a smile every day." - Anonymous

_____

_____

_____

_____

_____

_____

_____

_____

_____

_____

_____

_____

_____

_____

_____

_____

_____

_____

_____

_____

_____

_____

_____

About the Author

⤙⤚

⤙⤚

Margaret Martin has been on a life long journey of personal and professional development; and has found that writing down her gratitudes on a daily basis has added to her attitude of gratitude. Her mission is to help people to *"change your mindset to transform your life"* so they can experience a meaningful life of peace ~ joy ~ fulfillment. She is your *Means to Positive Change.*

As a Speaker | Coach | Author | Facilitator, Margaret has been providing her clients and followers the gift of helping them look at their life situations from a different perspective for over 20 years.

She lives in Dunedin, a wonderfully quaint town in the Tampa Bay area, where she in actively involved in her community.

You may reach Margaret:

Websites: www.MargaretMartin.com
Twitter: www.twitter.com/MargaretMartin
Facebook: www.facebook.com/MargaretMartin.SpeakerCoach
LinkedIn: http: www.linkedin.com/MargaretMartin
YouTube: www.youtube.com/user/MargaretMartinFL

Made in the USA
Columbia, SC
29 April 2018